The Bou...

and

The Garden of Adonis

from Book II and Book III of
The Fairy Queen

EDMUND SPENSER

A Phoenix Paperback

The Faerie Queene by Edmund Spenser first included in
Everyman's Library in 1987

This abridged and lightly modernised extract first published
in 1996 by Phoenix
a division of Orion Books Ltd
Orion House, 5 Upper St Martin's Lane, London WC2H 9EA

Copyright © Orion Books Ltd 1996

Cover illustration: The Rainbow Portrait of Elizabeth I, courtesy of the
Marquess of Salisbury, Hatfield House

ISBN 1 85799 675 5

Typeset in Sabon by Deltatype Ltd, Ellesmere Port, Cheshire
Printed in Great Britain by
Clays Ltd, St Ives plc

Contents

The Bower of Bliss
BOOK II, CANTO 12

Guyon, by Palmer's governance
   Passing through perils great,
Doth overthrow the Bower of Bliss
   And Acrasia defeat.

1

Now 'gins this goodly frame of Temperance
   Fairly to rise, and her adorned head
   To prick of highest praise forth to advance,
   Formerly grounded and fast settled
   On firm foundation of true bountihead;
   And this brave knight, that for virtue fights,
   Now comes to point of that same perilous stead,
   Where Pleasure dwells in sensual delights,
'Mongst thousand dangers, and ten thousand magic
   mights.

2

Two days now in that sea he sailed has,
   Ne ever land beheld, ne living wight,
   Ne ought save peril, still as he did pass.
   Tho, when appeared the third morrow bright

Upon the waves to spread her trembling light,
An hideous roaring far away they heard
That all their senses filled with affright,
And straight they saw the raging surges reared
Up to the skies, that them of drowning made afeared.

3

Said then the Boatman: 'Palmer, steer aright
And keep an even course; for yonder way
We needs must pass (God do us well acquit!).
That is the Gulf of Greediness, they say,
That deep engorgeth all this world's prey –
Which having swallowed up excessively,
He soon in vomit up again doth lay
And belcheth forth his superfluity,
That all the seas for fear do seem away to fly.

4

'On the other side an hideous rock is pight
Of mighty magnes stone, whose craggy clift
Depending from on high, dreadful to sight,
Over the waves his rugged arms doth lift
And threateneth down to throw his ragged rift
On whoso cometh nigh: yet nigh it draws
All passengers, that none from it can shift,
For whiles they fly that Gulf's devouring jaws
They on this rock are rent and sunk in helpless waves.'

5

Forward they pass and strongly he them rows
   Until they nigh unto that Gulf arrive,
   Where stream more violent and greedy grows.
   Then he with all his puissance doth strive
   To strike his oars, and mightily doth drive
   The hollow vessel through the threatful wave
   Which, gaping wide to swallow them alive
   In the huge abyss of his engulfing grave,
Doth roar at them in vain, and with great terror rave.

6

They, passing by, that grisly mouth did see
   Sucking the seas into his entrails deep
   That seemed more horrible than hell to be,
   Or that dark dreadful hole of Tartar' steep
   Through which the damned ghosts do often creep
   Back to the world, bad livers to torment –
   But nought that falls into this direful deep,
   Ne that approacheth nigh the wide descent,
May back return, but is condemned to be drent.

7

On the other side they saw that perilous rock
   Threatening itself on them to ruinate,
   On whose sharp cliffs the ribs of vessels broke,
   And shivered ships which had been wrecked late,
   Yet stuck, with carcases exanimate

Of such as, having all their substance spent
In wanton joys and lusts intemperate,
Did afterwards make shipwrack violent
Both of their life and fame, for ever foully blent.

8

For-thy this hight the Rock of Vile Reproach –
A dangerous and detestable place
To which nor fish nor fowl did once approach
But yelling mews with seagulls hoarse and base,
And cormorants with birds of ravenous race,
Which still sat waiting on that wasteful clift
For spoil of wretches, whose unhappy case –
After lost credit and consumed thrift –
At last them driven hath to this despairful drift.

9

The Palmer, seeing them in safety passed,
Thus said: 'behold the examples in our sights
Of lustful luxury and thriftless waste.
What now is left of miserable wights
Which spent their looser days in lewd delights
But shame and sad reproach, here to be read
By these rent relics speaking their ill plights?
Let all that live hereby be counselled
To shun Rock of Reproach, and it as death to dread.'

10

So forth they rowed, and that ferryman
  With his stiff oars did brush the sea so strong
  That the hoar waters from his frigate ran
  And the light bubbles danced all along
  Whiles the salt brine out of the billows sprang.
  At last far off, they many islands spy
  On every side floating the floods among.
  Then said the knight: 'Lo, I the land descry;
Therefore, old sire, thy course do thereunto apply.'

11

'That may not be,' said then the ferryman,
  'Lest we unweeting hap to be fordone;
  For those same islands, seeming now and then,
  Are not firm land, nor any certain wone,
  But straggling plots, which to and fro do run
  In the wide waters: therefore are they hight
  The Wandering Islands. Therefore do them shun,
  For they have oft drawn many a wandering wight
Into most deadly danger and distressed plight.

12

'Yet well they seem to him that far doth view –
  Both fair and fruitful, and the ground dispread
  With grassy green of delectable hue,
  And the tall trees, with leaves apparelled,
  Are decked with blossoms dyed in white and red

That mote the passengers thereto allure.
But whosoever once hath fastened
His foot thereon may never it recure,
But wandereth ever more uncertain and unsure:

13

'As the Isle of Delos whilom, men report,
Amid the Aegean Sea long time did stray,
Ne made for shipping any certain port
Till that Latona, travelling that way
Flying from Juno's wrath and hard assay,
Of her fair twins was there delivered
Which afterwards did rule the night and day:
Thenceforth it firmly was established,
And for Apollo's honour highly heried.'

14

They to him hearken as beseemeth meet,
And pass on forward: so their way does lie
That one of those same islands which do fleet
In the wide sea they needs must passen by –
Which seemed so sweet and pleasant to the eye,
That it would tempt a man to touchen there.
Upon the bank they sitting did espy
A dainty damsel dressing of her hair,
By whom a little skippet floating did appear.

She, them espying, loud to them can call,
    Bidding them nigher draw unto the shore,
    For she had cause to busy them withal;
    And therewith loudly laughed. But nathemore
    Would they once turn, but kept on as afore;
    Which, when she saw, she left her locks undight
    And, running to her boat withouten oar,
    From the departing land it launched light
And after them did drive with all her power and might.

Whom, overtaking, she in merry sort
    Them 'gan to board and purpose diversely,
    Now feigning dalliance and wanton sport,
    Now throwing forth lewd words immodestly,
    Till that the Palmer 'gan full bitterly
    Her to rebuke for being loose and light:
    Which not abiding, but more scornfully
    Scoffing at him that did her justly wite,
She turned her boat about and from them rowed quite.

That was the wanton Phaedria, which late
    Did ferry him over the Idle Lake;
    Whom, nought regarding, they kept on their gate
    And all her vain allurements did forsake,
    When them the wary boatman thus bespake:
    'Here now behoveth us well to advise

And of our safety good heed to take;
   For here before a perilous passage lies
Where many mermaids haunt, making false melodies.

18

'But by the way there is a great quicksand
   And whirlpool of hidden jeopardy:
   Therefore, Sir Palmer, keep an even hand,
   For 'twixt them both the narrow way doth lie.'
   Scarce had he said when, hard at hand, they spy
   That quicksand nigh with water covered;
   But by the checked wave they did descry
   It plain, and by the sea discoloured.
It called was the Quicksand of Unthriftihead.

19

They, passing by, a goodly ship did see,
   Laden from far with precious merchandise
   And bravely furnished as ship might be,
   Which, through great disadventure or misprize,
   Herself had run into that hazardise;
   Whose mariners and merchants, with much toil,
   Laboured in vain to have recured their prize
   And the rich wares to save from piteous spoil.
But neither toil nor travail might her back recoil.

20

On the other side they see that perilous pool
   That called was the Whirlpool of Decay

(In which full many had with hapless dole
  Been sunk, of whom no memory did stay),
  Whose circled waters, rapt with swirling sway
  Like to a restless wheel, still running round,
  Did covet, as they passed by that way,
  To draw their boat within the utmost bound
Of his wide labyrinth, and then to have them drowned.

21

But the heedful boatman strongly forth did stretch
  His brawny arms and all his body strain
  That the utmost sandy breach they shortly fetch,
  Whiles the dread danger does behind remain.
  Sudden they see, from midst of all the main,
  The surging waters like a mountain rise,
  And the great sea puffed up with proud disdain
  To swell above the measure of his guise
As threatening to devour all that his power despise.

22

The waves came rolling, and the billows roar
  Outrageously, as they enraged were,
  Or wrathful Neptune did them drive before
  His whirling chariot, for exceeding fear
  (For not one puff of wind there did appear);
  That all the three thereat wox much afraid,
  Unweeting what such horror strange did rear.

Eftsoons they saw an hideous host arrayed
Of huge sea monsters, such as living sense dismayed.

23

Most ugly shapes and horrible aspects,
　　Such as Dame Nature self mote fear to see,
　　Or shame that ever should so foul defects
　　From her most cunning hand escaped be –
　　All dreadful portraits of deformity:
　　Spring-headed hydras and sea-shouldering whales;
　　Great whirlpools (which all fishes make to flee);
　　Bright scolopendras armed with silver scales;
Mighty monceroses with immeasured tails;

24

The dreadful fish that hath deserved the name
　　Of death, and like him looks in dreadful hue;
　　The grisly wasserman, that makes his game
　　The flying ships with swiftness to pursue;
　　The horrible sea-satyr, that doth show
　　His fearful face in time of greatest storm;
　　Huge ziffius, whom mariners eschew
　　No less than rocks (as travellers inform);
And greedy rosmarines with visages deform.

25

All these and thousands thousands many more,
　　And more deformed monsters thousand fold,

With dreadful noise and hollow rumbling roar
Came rushing in the foamy waves enrolled,
Which seemed to fly for fear them to behold:
No wonder if these did the knight appall;
For all that here on earth we dreadful hold
Be but as bugs to fearen babes withal
Compared to the creatures in the sea's entrail.

26

'Fear nought,' then said the Palmer well-advised,
'For these same monsters are not these indeed,
But are into these fearful shapes disguised
By that same wicked witch to work us dread,
And draw from on this journey to proceed.'
Tho, lifting up his virtuous staff on high,
He smote the sea, which calmed was with speed;
And all that dreadful army fast 'gan fly
Into great Tethys' bosom, where they hidden lie.

27

Quit from that danger forth their course they kept,
And as they went they heard a rueful cry
Of one, that wailed and pitifully wept
That through the sea resounding plaints did fly.
At last they in an island did espy
A seemly maiden, sitting by the shore,
That with great sorrow and sad agony,
Seemed some great misfortune to deplore,
And loud to them for succour called evermore:

Which Guyon, hearing, straight the Palmer bade
  To steer the boat towards that doleful maid
  That he might know, and ease, her sorrow sad;
  Who him, advising better, to him said:
  'Fair sir, be not displeased if disobeyed,
  For ill it were to hearken to her cry;
  For she is inly nothing ill apaid,
  But only womanish fine forgery
Your stubborn heart to affect with frail infirmity.

'To which, when she your courage hath inclined
  Through foolish pity, then her guileful bait
  She will embosom deeper in your mind
  And for your ruin at the last await.'
  The knight was ruled, and the boatman straight
  Held on his course with staid steadfastness,
  Ne ever shrunk, ne ever sought to bate
  His tired arms for toiled weariness,
But with his oars did sweep the watery wilderness.

And now they nigh approached to the stead
  Whereas those mermaids dwelt. It was a still
  And calmy bay, on the one side sheltered
  With the broad shadow of an hoary hill;

On the other side an high rock towered still,
    That 'twixt them both a pleasant port they made
    And did like an half theatre fulfil.
    There those five sisters had continual trade
And used to bath themselves in that deceitful shade.

                              31
They were fair ladies till they fondly strived
    With the Heliconian maids for mastery –
    Of whom they, overcomen, were deprived
    Of their proud beauty and the one moiety
    Transformed to fish for their bold surquedry,
    But the upper half their hue retained still
    And their sweet skill in wonted melody,
    Which ever after they abused to ill
To allure weak travellers whom, gotten, they did kill.

                              32
So now to Guyon, as he passed by,
    Their pleasant tunes they sweetly thus applied:
    'O thou, fair son of gentle fairy,
    That art in mighty arms most magnified
    Above all knights that ever battle tried,
    O turn thy rudder hitherward awhile.
    Here may thy storm-beat vessel safely ride –
    This is the port of rest from troublous toil,
The world's sweet inn from pain and wearisome turmoil.'

With that the rolling sea, resounding soft,
    In his big bass them fitly answered;
    And on the rock the waves, breaking aloft,
    A solemn mean unto them measured,
    The whiles sweet Zephyrus loud whistled
    His treble – a strange kind of harmony
    Which Guyon's senses softly tickled
    That he the boatman bade row easily
And let him hear some part of their rare melody.

But him the Palmer from that vanity
    With temperate advice discounselled
    That they it passed, and shortly 'gan descry
    The land to which their course they levelled;
    When suddenly a gross fog overspread,
    With his dull vapour, all that desert has,
    And heaven's cheerful face enveloped,
    That all things one, and one as nothing, was,
And this great universe seemed one confused mass.

Thereat they greatly were dismayed, ne wist
    How to direct their way in darkness wide,
    But feared to wander in that wasteful mist
    For tumbling into mischief unespied:
Worse is the danger hidden than descried.

Suddenly an innumerable flight
   Of harmful fowls, about them fluttering, cried,
   And with their wicked wings them oft did smite
And sore annoyed, groping in that grisly night.

36

Even all the nation of unfortunate
   And fatal birds about them flocked were,
   Such as, by nature, men abhor and hate:
   The ill-faced owl, death's dreadful messenger;
   The hoarse night-raven, trump of doleful drear;
   The leather-winged bat, day's enemy;
   The rueful stritch, still waiting on the bier;
   The whistler shrill, that whoso hears doth die;
The hellish harpies, prophets of sad destiny.

37

All those, and all that else doth horror breed,
   About them flew, and filled their sails with fear.
   Yet stayd they not, but forward did proceed,
   Whiles the one did row, and the other stiffly steer,
   Till that at last the weather 'gan to clear
   And the fair land itself did plainly show.
   Said then the Palmer: 'Lo where does appear
   The sacred soil where all our perils grow:
Therefore, sir knight, your ready arms about you throw.'

He hearkened, and his arms about him took,
 The whiles the nimble boat so well her sped
 That with her crooked keel the land she struck.
 Then forth the noble Guyon sallied,
 And his sage Palmer that him governed;
 But the other by his boat behind did stay.
 They marched fairly forth, of nought ydread,
 Both firmly armed for every hard assay,
With constancy and care, 'gainst danger and dismay.

Ere long they heard an hideous bellowing
 Of many beasts that roared outrageously
 As if that hunger's point, or Venus' sting,
 Had them enraged with fell surquedry.
 Yet nought they feared, but passed on hardily
 Until they came in view of those wild beasts
 Who, all at once, gaping full greedily,
 And rearing fiercely their upstarting crests,
Ran towards to devour those unexpected guests.

But soon as they approached with deadly threat
 The Palmer over them his staff upheld –
 His mighty staff that could all charms defeat.
 Eftsoons their stubborn courages were quelled
 And high-advanced crests down meekly felled.
 Instead of fraying, they themselves did fear,

And trembled as them passing they beheld,
  Such wondrous power did in that staff appear
All monsters to subdue to him that did it bear.

41

Of that same wood it framed was cunningly
  Of which Caduceus whilom was made –
  Caduceus the rod of Mercury,
  With which he wonts the Stygian realms invade
  Through ghastly horror and eternal shade.
  The infernal fiends with it he can assuage,
  And Orcus tame, whom nothing can persuade,
  And rule the Furies when they most do rage:
Such virtue in his staff had eke this Palmer sage.

42

Thence passing forth, they shortly do arrive
  Whereas the Bower of Bliss was situate –
  A place picked out by choice of best alive
  That Nature's work by art can imitate;
  In which whatever in this worldly state
  Is sweet and pleasing unto living sense,
  Or that may daintiest fantasy aggrate,
  Was poured forth with plentifull dispence
And made there to abound with lavish affluence.

43

Goodly it was enclosed round about,
  As well their entered guests to keep within

As those unruly beasts to hold without –
Yet was the fence thereof but weak and thin:
Nought feared their force that fortalage to win,
But wisdom's power, and temperance's might,
By which the mightiest things efforced been.
And eke the gate was wrought of substance light,
Rather for pleasure then for battery or fight:

44

It framed was of precious ivory,
　　That seemed a work of admirable wit.
　　And therein all the famous history
　　Of Jason and Medea was ywrit:
　　Her mighty charms, her furious loving fit;
　　His goodly conquest of the golden fleece,
　　His falsed faith and love too lightly flit;
　　The wondered Argo, which in venturous piece
First through the Euxine seas bore all the flower of Greece.

45

Ye might have seen the frothy billows fry
　　Under the ship as through them she went,
　　That seemed the waves were into ivory –
　　Or ivory into the waves – were sent;
　　And otherwhere the snowy substance sprent
　　With vermil, like the boy's blood therein shed,
　　A piteous spectacle did represent;
　　And otherwhiles, with gold besprinkled,
It seemed the enchanted flame which did Creusa wed.

All this, and more, might from that goodly gate
  Be read, that ever open stood to all
  Which thither came. But in the porch there sat
  A comely personage, of stature tall
  And semblance pleasing more than natural,
  That travellers to him seemed to entice:
  His looser garment to the ground did fall
  And flew about his heels in wanton wise,
Not fit for speedy pace or manly exercise.

They in that place him Genius did call:
  Not that celestial power to whom the care
  Of life and generation of all
  That lives pertains in charge particular
  (Who wondrous things concerning our welfare,
  And strange phantoms doth let us oft foresee,
  And oft of secret ills bids us beware:
  That is ourself, whom, though we do not see,
Yet each doth in himself it well perceive to be;

Therefore a god him sage antiquity
  Did wisely make, and good Agdistis call);
  But this same was to that quite contrary –
  The foe of life, that good envies to all,

That secretly doth us procure to fall
Through guileful semblants which he makes us see.
He of this garden had the governail,
And Pleasure's porter was devised to be,
Holding a staff in hand for more formality.

49

With diverse flowers he daintily was decked
And strewed about, and by his side
A mighty mazer bowl of wine was set
As if it had been sacrified,
Wherewith all new-come guests he gratified.
So did he eke Sir Guyon, passing by;
But he his idle courtesy defied,
And overthrew his bowl disdainfully,
And broke his staff, with which he charmed semblants sly.

50

Thus being entered, they behold around
A large and spacious plain, on every side
Strewed with pleasances, whose fair grassy ground,
Mantled with green, and goodly beautified
With all the ornaments of Flora's pride,
Wherewith her mother, Art, as half in scorn
Of niggard Nature, like a pompous bride
Did deck her and too lavishly adorn,
When forth from virgin bower she comes in the early morn.

Thereto the heavens, always jovial,
   Looked on them lovely, still in steadfast state,
   Ne suffered storm nor frost on them to fall,
   Their tender buds or leaves to violate;
   Nor scorching heat, nor cold intemperate
   To afflict the creatures which therein did dwell;
   But the mild air with season moderate
   Gently attempered and disposed so well
That still it breathed forth sweet spirit and wholesome
   smell:

More sweet and wholesome than the pleasant hill
   Of Rhodope, on which the nymph that bore
   A giant babe herself for grief did kill;
   Or the Thessalian Tempe, where of yore
   Fair Daphne Phoebus' heart with love did gore;
   Or Ida, where the gods loved to repair
   Wherever they their heavenly bowers forlore;
   Or sweet Parnass', the haunt of Muses fair;
Or Eden self, if aught with Eden mote compare.

Much wondered Guyon at the fair aspect
   Of that sweet place, yet suffered no delight
   To sink into his sense nor mind affect,
   But passed forth and looked still forward right,

Bridling his will and mastering his might,
Till that he came unto another gate –
No gate, but like one, being goodly dight
With boughs and branches, which did broad dilate
Their clasping arms in wanton wreathings intricate,

54

So fashioned a porch with rare device,
 Arched overhead with an embracing vine,
 Whose bunches hanging down, seemed to entice
 All passers by to taste their luscious wine,
 And did themselves into their hands incline,
 As freely offering to be gathered:
 Some deep empurpled, as the Hyacinth;
 Some as the rubine, laughing sweetly red;
Some like fair emeralds, not yet well ripened.

55

And them amongst some were of burnished gold –
 So made by art to beautify the rest –
 Which did themselves amongst the leaves enfold,
 As lurking from the view of covetous guest
 That the weak boughs, with so rich load oppressed,
 Did bow adown as over-burdened.
 Under that porch a comely dame did rest,
 Clad in fair weeds but foul disordered,
And garments loose that seemed unfit for womanhead.

In her left hand a cup of gold she held,
  And with her right the riper fruit did reach,
  Whose sappy liquor – that with fulness swelled –
  Into her cup she scruzed, with dainty breach
  Of her fine fingers, without foul impeach,
  That so fair wine press made the wine more sweet:
  Thereof she used to give to drink to each
  Whom, passing by, she happened to meet:
It was her guise all strangers goodly so to greet.

So she to Guyon offered it to taste,
  Who, taking it out of her tender hand,
  The cup to ground did violently cast
  That all in pieces it was broken found,
  And with the liquor stained all the land.
  Whereat Excess exceedingly was wroth,
  Yet n'ote the same amend, ne yet withstand,
  But suffered him to pass, all were she loath –
Who, nought regarding her displeasure, forward goeth.

There the most dainty paradise on ground
  Itself doth offer to his sober eye,
  In which all pleasures plenteously abound,
  And none does other's happiness envy:
  The painted flowers, the trees upshooting high,

The dales for shade, the hills for breathing space,
  The trembling groves, the crystal running by,
  And that which all fair works doth most aggrace,
That Art, which all that wrought, appeared in no place.

59

One would have thought (so cunningly the rude
  And scorned parts were mingled with the fine)
  That Nature had for wantoness, ensued
  Art, and that Art at Nature did repine:
  So striving each the other to undermine,
  Each did the other's work more beautify;
  So, differing both in wills, agreed in fine;
  So all agreed through sweet diversity,
This garden to adorn with all variety.

60

And in the midst of all a fountain stood,
  Of richest substance that on earth might be,
  So pure and shiny, that the silver flood
  Through every channel running one might see.
  Most goodly it with curious imagery
  Was overwrought, and shapes of naked boys –
  Of which some seemed with lively jollity
  To fly about, playing their wanton toys,
While others did themselves embay in liquid joys.

And, over all, of purest gold, was spread
    A trail of ivy in his native hue;
    For the rich metal was so coloured
    That wight who did not well-advised it view,
    Would surely deem it to be ivy true:
    Low his lascivious arms adown did creep
    That, themselves dipping in the silver dew,
    Their fleecy flowers they tenderly did steep,
Which drops of crystal seemed for wantonness to weep.

Infinite streams continually did well
    Out of this fountain, sweet and fair to see,
    The which into an ample laver fell
    And shortly grew to so great quantity
    That like a little lake it seemed to be,
    Whose depth exceeded not three cubits height,
    That through the waves one might the bottom see
    All paved with jasper shining bright,
That seemed the fountain in that sea did sail upright.

And all the margent round about was set
    With shady laurel trees, thence to defend
    The sunny beams which on the billows beat
    And those which therein bathed mote offend.
    As Guyon happened by the same to wend,

Two naked damsels he therein espied
    Which, therein bathing, seemed to contend
    And wrestle wantonly, ne cared to hide
Their dainty parts from view of any which them eyed.

Sometimes the one would lift the other quite
    Above the waters, and then down again
    Her plunge, as overmastered by might,
    Where both awhile would covered remain,
    And each the other from to rise restrain –
    The whiles their snowy limbs, as through a veil,
    So through the crystal waves appeared plain;
    Then suddenly both would themselves unhele
And the amorous sweet spoils to greedy eyes reveal.

As that fair star, the messenger of morn,
    His dewy face out of the sea doth rear;
    Or as the Cyprian goddess, newly born
    Of the ocean's fruitful froth, did first appear:
    Such seemed they; and so their yellow hair
    Crystalline humour dropped down apace.
    Whom such, when Guyon saw, he drew him near,
    And somewhat 'gan relent his earnest pace:
His stubborn breast 'gan secret pleasance to embrace.

The wanton maids, him espying, stood
   Gazing awhile at his unwonted guise.
   Then the one herself low ducked in the flood,
   Abashed that her a stranger did advise;
   But the other rather higher did arise
   And her two lily paps aloft displayed,
   And all, that might his melting heart entice
   To her delights she unto him bewrayed
(The rest, hid underneath, him more desirous made).

With that, the other likewise thus uprose,
   And her fair locks – which formerly were bound
   Up in one knot – she low adown did loose,
   Which flowing low and thick, her clothed around
   And the ivory in golden mantle gowned.
   So that fair spectacle from him was reft,
   Yet that which reft it no less fair was found.
   So, hid in locks and waves from looker's theft,
Nought but her lovely face she for his looking left.

Withal she laughed, and she blushed withal,
   That blushing to her laughter gave more grace,
   And laughter to her blushing, as did fall.
   Now, when they spied the knight to slack his pace
   Them to behold, and in his sparkling face

The secret signs of kindled lust appear,
Their wanton merriments they did increase,
And to him beckoned, to approach more near,
And showed him many sights that courage cold could rear.

69

On which when gazing him the Palmer saw,
He much rebuked those wandering eyes of his
And, counselled well, him forward thence did draw.
Now are they come nigh to the Bower of Bliss –
Of her fond favourites so named amiss –
When thus the Palmer: 'Now, sir, well advise,
For here the end of all our travail is;
Here wones Acrasia, whom we must surprise
Else she will slip away, and all our drift despise.'

70

Eftsoons they heard a most melodious sound
Of all that mote delight a dainty ear –
Such as at once might not on living ground
(Save in this paradise) be heard elsewhere.
Right hard it was for wight which did it hear
To read what manner music that mote be;
For all that pleasing is to living ear
Was there consorted in one harmony –
Birds, voices, instruments, winds, waters, all agree.

The joyous birds, shrouded in cheerful shade,
   Their notes unto the voice attempered sweet;
   The angelical, soft trembling voices made
   To the instruments divine respondence meet;
   The silver-sounding instruments did meet
   With the bass murmur of the water's fall;
   The water's fall, with difference discrete –
   Now soft, now loud, unto the wind did call;
The gentle, warbling wind low answered to all.

There, whence that music seemed heard to be,
   Was the fair witch, herself now solacing
   With the new lover whom, through sorcery
   And witchcraft, she from far did thither bring.
   There she had him now laid slumbering
   In secret shade after long wanton joys,
   Whilst round about them pleasantly did sing
   Many fair ladies and lascivious boys,
That ever mixed their song with light licentious toys.

And all that while right over him she hung
   With her false eyes fast fixed in his sight,
   As seeking medicine whence she was stung,
   Or greedily depasturing delight;
   And, oft inclining down, with kisses light

(For fear of waking him) his lips bedewed,
And through his humid eyes did suck his sprite,
Quite molten into lust and pleasure lewd –
Wherewith she sighed oft as if his case she rued –

74

The whiles someone did chant this lovely lay:
  'Ah, see – who so fair thing dost fain to see –
In springing flower the image of thy day;
Ah, see the virgin rose, how sweetly she
Doth first peep forth with bashful modesty,
That fairer seems the less ye see her may.
Lo, see soon after how more bold and free
Her bared bosom she doth broad display;
Lo, see soon after how she fades and falls away.

75

'So passeth, in the passing of a day,
  Of mortal life the leaf, the bud, the flower,
Ne more doth flourish after first decay
That erst was sought to deck both bed and bower
Of many a lady and many a paramour:
Gather, therefore, the rose whilst yet is prime,
For soon comes age that will her pride deflower;
Gather the rose of love whilst yet is time,
Whilst loving thou mayest loved be with equal crime.'

He ceased, and then 'gan all the choir of birds
   Their diverse notes to attune unto his lay
   As in approvance of his pleasing words.
   The constant pair heard all that he did say,
   Yet swerved not, but kept their forward way
   Through many covert groves and thickets close,
   In which they, creeping, did at last display
   The wanton lady with her lover loose,
Whose sleepy head she in her lap did soft dispose.

Upon a bed of roses she was laid,
   As faint through heat, or dight to pleasant sin,
   And was arrayed – or, rather, disarrayed,
   All in a veil of silk and silver thin
   That hid no whit her alabaster skin,
   But rather showed more white, if more might be.
   More subtile web Arachne cannot spin,
   Nor the fine nets which oft we woven see
Of scorched dew, do not in the air more lightly flee.

Her snowy breast was bare to ready spoil
   Of hungry eyes, which n'ote therewith be filled,
   And yet, through languor of her late sweet toil,
   Few drops, more clear than nectar, forth distilled
   That like pure orient pearls adown it trilled,

And her fair eyes, sweet smiling in delight,
    Moistened their fiery beams, with which she thrilled
    Frail hearts, yet quenched not: like starry light
Which, sparkling on the silent waves, does seem more
    bright.

79

The young man sleeping by her seemed to be
    Some goodly swain of honourable place
    That certes it great pity was to see
    Him his nobility so foul deface:
    A sweet regard and amiable grace,
    Mixed with manly sternness, did appear,
    Yet sleeping, in his well-proportioned face,
    And on his tender lips the downy hair
Did now but freshly spring and silken blossoms bear.

80

His warlike arms – the idle instruments
    Of sleeping praise – were hung upon a tree,
    And his brave shield, full of old monuments,
    Was foully razed that none the signs might see.
    Ne for them ne for honour cared he,
    Ne aught that did to his advancement tend,
    But in lewd loves and wasteful luxury
    His days, his goods, his body he did spend:
O horrible enchantment that him so did blend.

The noble elf and careful Palmer drew
  So nigh to them (minding nought but lustful game)
  That sudden forth they on them rushed, and threw
  A subtle net which only for the same
  The skilful Palmer formally did frame.
  So held them under fast, the whiles the rest
  Fled all away for fear of fouller shame.
  The fair Enchantress, so unwares oppressed,
Tried all her arts, and all her sleights, thence out to wrest.

And eke her lover strove, but all in vain:
  For that same net so cunningly was wound
  That neither guile nor force might it distrain.
  They took them both, and both them strongly bound
  In captive bands which there they ready found;
  But her in chains of adamant he tied,
  For nothing else might keep her safe and sound;
  But Verdant (so he hight) he soon untied,
And counsel sage instead thereof to him applied.

But all those pleasant bowers and palaces brave
  Guyon broke down with rigour pitiless,
  Ne aught their goodly workmanship might save
  Them from the tempest of his wrathfulness
  But that their bliss he turned to balefulness.

Their groves he felled, their gardens did deface,
Their arbours spoil, their cabinets suppress,
Their banquet houses burn, their buildings raze,
And of the fairest late now made the foulest place.

84

Then led they her away, and eke that knight
    They with them led, both sorrowful and sad.
    The way they came, the same returned they right,
    Till they arrived where they lately had
    Charmed those wild beasts that raged with fury mad –
    Which, now awaking, fierce at them 'gan fly
    As in their mistress's rescue whom they led;
    But them the Palmer soon did pacify.
Then Guyon asked, what meant those beasts which there
    did lie.

85

Said he: 'These seeming beasts are men indeed
    Whom this enchantress hath transformed thus –
    Whilom her lovers which her lusts did feed,
    Now turned into figures hideous
    According to their minds like monstrous.'
    'Sad end' (quoth he) 'of life intemperate,
    And mournful meed of joys delicious:
    But, Palmer, if it mote thee so aggrate,
Let them returned be unto their former state.'

86

Straightway he with his virtuous staff them struck,
    And straight of beasts they comely men became:
    Yet, being men, they did unmanly look,
    And stared ghastly, some for inward shame,
    And some for wrath, to see their captive dame.
    But one above the rest in special,
    That had an hog been late – hight Grill by name –
    Repined greatly, and did him miscall
That had from hoggish form him brought to natural.

87

Said Guyon: 'See the mind of beastly man
    That hath so soon forgot the excellence
    Of his creation when he life began,
    That now he chooseth, with vile difference,
    To be a beast and lack intelligence.'
    To whom the Palmer thus: 'The dunghill kind
    Delights in filth and foul incontinence:
    Let Grill be Grill and have his hoggish mind;
But let us hence depart whilst weather serves, and wind.'

The Garden of Adonis

BOOK III, CANTO 6

The birth of fair Belphoebe and
    Of Amoret is told.
The garden of Adonis fraught
    With pleasures manifold.

1

Well may I ween, fair ladies, all this while
    Ye wonder how this noble damosel
So great perfections did in her compile,
    Sith that in savage forests she did dwell,
    So far from court and royal citadel,
    The great schoolmistress of all courtesy:
Seemeth that such wild woods should far expel
    All civil usage and gentility,
And gentle sprite deform with rude rusticity.

2

But to this fair Belphoebe in her birth
    The heavens so favourable were and free,
    Looking with mild aspect upon the earth,
    In the horoscope of her nativity,
    That all the gifts of grace and chastity

On her they poured forth of plenteous horn:
Jove laughed on Venus from his sovereign see,
And Phoebus with fair beams did her adorn,
And all the Graces rocked her cradle, being born.

3

Her birth was of the womb of morning dew,
    And her conception of the joyous prime,
    And all her whole creation did her show
    Pure and unspotted from all loathly crime
    That is ingenerate in fleshly slime.
    So was this virgin born, so was she bred,
    So was she trained up from time to time
    In all chaste virtue and true bountihead
Till to her due perfection she was ripened.

4

Her mother was the fair Chrysogone,
    The daughter of Amphisa, who by race
    A fairy was, yborn of high degree:
    She bore Belphoebe; she bore in like case
    Fair Amoretta in the second place.
    These two were twins, and twixt them two did share
    The heritage of all celestial grace
    That all the rest it seemed they robbed bare
Of bounty, and of beauty, and all virtues rare.

5

It were a goodly story to declare
  By what strange accident fair Chrysogone
  Conceived these infants, and how them she bare
  In this wild forest, wandering all alone,
  After she had nine months fulfilled and gone.
  For not as other women's common brood
  They were enwombed in the sacred throne
  Of her chaste body, nor with common food,
As other women's babies, they sucked vital blood.

6

But wondrously they were begot and bred
  Through influence of the heavens' fruitful ray,
  As it in antique books is mentioned:
  It was upon a summer's shiny day,
  When Titan fair his beams did display,
  In a fresh fountain, far from all men's view,
  She bathed her breast the boiling heat to allay.
  She bathed with roses red, and violets blue,
And all the sweetest flowers that in the forest grew.

7

Till, faint through irksome weariness, adown
  Upon the grassy ground herself she laid
  To sleep, the whiles a gentle slumbering swoon
  Upon her fell, all naked bare displayed.
  The sunbeams bright upon her body played,

Being through former bathing mollified,
And pierced into her womb, where they embayed
With so sweet sense and secret power unspied
That in her pregnant flesh they shortly fructified.

8

Miraculous may seem to him that reads
    So strange example of conception;
    But reason teacheth that the fruitful seeds
    Of all things living, through impression
    Of the sunbeams in moist complexion,
    Do life conceive and quickened are by kind:
    So after Nilus' inundation,
    Infinite shapes of creatures men do find,
Informed in the mud on which the sun hath shined.

9

Great father, he, of generation
    Is rightly called, the author of life and light;
    And his fair sister for creation
    Ministreth matter fit which, tempered right
    With heat and humour, breeds the living wight.
    So sprang these twins in womb of Chrysogone;
    Yet wist she nought thereof but, sore affright,
    Wondered to see her belly so upblown,
Which still increased till she her term had full outgone.

Whereof conceiving shame and foul disgrace
   (Albe her guiltless conscience her cleared),
   She fled into the wilderness a space
   Till that unwieldy burden she had reared,
   And shunned dishonour, which as death she feared;
   Where, weary of long travail, down to rest
   Herself she set, and comfortably cheered.
   There a sad cloud of sleep her overcast
And seized every sense with sorrow sore oppressed.

11

It fortuned fair Venus, having lost
   Her little son, the winged god of love
   (Who, for some light displeasure which him crossed,
   Was from her fled as flit as airy dove,
   And left her blissful bower of joy above –
   So from her often he had fled away
   When she for aught him sharply did reprove,
   And wandered in the world in strange array,
Disguised in many shapes that none might him bewray),

12

Him for to seek she left her heavenly house –
   The house of goodly forms and fair aspects
   Whence all the world derives the glorious
   Features of beauty, and all shapes select,
   With which high God his workmanship hath decked –

And searched every way through which his wings
  Had borne him or his track she mote detect:
  She promised kisses sweet, and sweeter things
Unto the man that of him tidings to her brings.

13

First she him sought in court, where most he used
  Whilom to haunt, but there she found him not;
  But many there she found which sore accused
  His falsehood, and with foul, infamous blot
  His cruel deeds and wicked wiles did spot:
  Ladies and lords she everywhere mote hear
  Complaining how, with his empoisoned shot,
  Their woeful hearts he wounded had whilere,
And so had left them languishing 'twixt hope and fear.

14

She then the cities sought from gate to gate,
  And everyone did ask, did he him see?
  And everyone her answered that too late
  He had him seen, and felt the cruelty
  Of his sharp darts and hot artillery;
  And everyone threw forth reproaches rife
  Of his mischievous deeds, and said that he
  Was the disturber of all civil life,
The enemy of peace, and author of all strife.

15

Then in the country she abroad him sought,
  And in the rural cottages inquired,
  Where also many plaints to her were brought
  How he their heedless hearts with love had fired,
  And his false venom through their veins inspired.
  And eke the gentle shepherd swains, which sat
  Keeping their fleecy flocks, as they were hired,
  She sweetly heard complain both how and what
Her son had to them done – yet she did smile thereat.

16

But when in none of all these she him got,
  She 'gan advise where else he mote him hide.
  At last she her bethought that she had not
  Yet sought the savage woods and forests wide
  In which full many lovely nymphs abide,
  'Mongst whom might be that he did closely lie,
  Or that the love of some of them him tied:
  For-thy she thither cast her course to apply
To search the secret haunts of Dian's company.

17

Shortly unto the wasteful woods she came,
  Whereas she found the goddess with her crew,
  After late chase of their imbrued game,
  Sitting beside a fountain in a row –
  Some of them washing with the liquid dew

From off their dainty limbs the dusty sweat
And soil which did deform their lively hue;
Others lay shaded from the scorching heat;
The rest upon her person gave attendance great.

18

She, having hung upon a bough on high
    Her bow and painted quiver, had unlaced
    Her silver buskins from her nimble thigh,
    And her lank loins ungirt, and breasts unbraced,
    After her heat the breathing cold to taste.
    Her golden locks – that late in tresses bright
    Embraided were for hindering of her haste –
    Now loose about her shoulders hung undight,
And were with sweet ambrosia all besprinkled light.

19

Soon as she Venus saw behind her back
    She was ashamed to be so loose surprised,
    And wox half wroth against her damsels slack
    That had not her thereof before advised,
    But suffered her so carelessly disguised
    Be overtaken. Soon her garments loose
    Upgathering, in her bosom she comprised
    Well as she might, and to the Goddess rose,
Whiles all her nymphs did like a garland her enclose.

20

Goodly she 'gan fair Cytherea greet,
  And shortly asked her what cause her brought
  Into that wilderness, for her unmeet,
  From her sweet bowers and beds with pleasures
    fraught –
  That sudden change she strange adventure thought.
  To whom half-weeping, she thus answered
  That she her dearest son Cupido sought
  Who, in his frowardness, from her was fled;
That she repented sore to have him angered.

21

Thereat Diana 'gan to smile in scorn
  Of her vain 'plaint, and to her, scoffing, said:
  'Great pity, sure, that ye be so forlorn
  Of your gay son that gives ye so good aid
  To your disports: ill mote ye been apaid.'
  But she was more engrieved, and replied:
  'Fair sister, ill beseems it to upbraid
  A doleful heart with so disdainful pride:
The like that mine, may be your pain another tide.

22

As you in woods and wanton wilderness
  Your glory set to chase the savage beasts,
  So my delight is all in joyfulness –
  In beds, in bowers, in banquets and in feasts;

And ill becomes you, with your lofty crests,
    To scorn the joy that Jove is glad to seek.
    We both are bound to follow heaven's behests,
    And tend our charges with obeisance meek:
Spare, gentle sister, with reproach my pain to eke,

23

'And tell me if that ye my son have heard
    To lurk amongst your nymphs in secret wise,
    Or keep their cabins. Much am I afeared
    Lest he like one of them himself disguise
    And turn his arrows to their exercise –
    So may he long himself full easy hide,
    For he is fair and fresh in face and guise
    As any nymph (let it not be envied).'
So saying, every nymph full narrowly she eyed.

24

But Phoebe therewith sore was angered,
    And sharply said: 'Go, dame – go seek your boy
    Where you him left, in Mars's bed.
    He comes not here – we scorn his foolish joy,
    Ne lend we leisure to his idle toy.
    But if I catch him in this company,
    By Stygian lake I vow – whose sad annoy
    The gods do dread – he dearly shall aby:
I'll clip his wanton wings that he no more shall fly.'

Whom whenas Venus saw so sore displeased,
   She inly sorry was and 'gan relent
   What she had said: so her she soon appeased
   With sugared words and gentle blandishment
   Which, as a fountain, from her sweet lips went
   And welled goodly forth that, in short space,
   She was well pleased and forth her damsels sent
   Through all the woods to search from place to place
If any track of him or tidings they mote trace.

To search the god of love her nymphs she sent
   Throughout the wandering forest everywhere;
   And after them herself eke with her went
   To seek the fugitive both far and near.
   So long they sought till they arrived were
   In that same shady covert whereas lay
   Fair Chrysogone in slumbery trance whilere –
   Who, in her sleep (a wondrous thing to say),
Unwares had born two babes as fair as springing day.

Unwares she them conceived, unwares she bore:
   She bore withouten pain that she conceived
   Withouten pleasure – ne her need implore
   Lucina's aid. Which, when they both perceived,
   They were through wonder nigh of sense bereaved

And, gazing each on other, nought bespake.
    At last they both agreed, her seeming grieved,
    Out of her heavy swoon not to awake
But from her loving side the tender babes to take.

28

Up they them took – each one a babe uptook –
    And with them carried to be fostered.
    Dame Phoebe to a nymph her babe betook
    To be upbrought in perfect maidenhead,
    And of herself her name Belphoebe read;
    But Venus hers thence far away conveyed
    To be upbrought in goodly womanhead,
    And in her little love's stead, which was strayed,
Her Amoret called, to comfort her dismayed.

29

She brought her to her joyous paradise
    Where most she wones when she on earth does dwell –
    So fair a place as Nature can devise:
    Whether in Paphos, or Cytheron hill,
    Or it in Gnidus be, I wote not well.
    But well I wote by trial that this same
    All other pleasant places doth excel,
    And called is by her lost lover's name
The Garden of Adonis, far renowned by fame.

In that same garden all the goodly flowers
   Wherewith Dame Nature doth her beautify,
   And decks the garlands of her paramours,
   Are fetched. There is the first seminary
   Of all things that are born to live and die
   According to their kinds. Long work it were
   Here to account the endless progeny
   Of all the weeds that bud and blossom there:
But so much as doth need must needs be counted here.

It sited was in fruitful soil of old,
   And girt in with two walls on either side,
   The one of iron, the other of bright gold,
   That none might through break nor overstride.
   And double gates it had which opened wide
   By which both in and out men moten pass –
   The one fair and fresh, the other old and dried.
   Old Genius the porter of them was –
Old Genius, the which a double nature has.

He letteth in, he letteth out to wend
   All that to come into the world desire:
   A thousand thousand naked babes attend
   About him day and night, which do require
   That he with fleshly weeds would them attire.

Such as him list, such as eternal Fate
   Ordained hath, he clothes with sinful mire
   And sendeth forth to live in mortal state
Till they again return back by the hinder gate.

33

After that they again returned been,
   They in that garden planted be again
   And grow afresh, as they had never seen
   Fleshly corruption nor mortal pain.
   Some thousand years so doen they there remain,
   And then of him are clad with other hue,
   Or sent into the changeful world again
   Till thither they return where first they grew:
So like a wheel around they run from old to new.

34

Ne needs there gardener to set or sow,
   To plant or prune for, of their own accord,
   All things as they created were do grow,
   And yet remember well the mighty word
   Which first was spoken by the Almighty lord
   That bade them to increase and multiply.
   No do they need with water of the ford
   Or of the clouds to moisten their roots dry,
For in themselves eternal moisture they imply.

Infinite shapes of creatures there are bred,
   And uncouth forms which none yet ever knew,
   And every sort is in a sundry bed
   Set by itself and ranked in comely row:
   Some fit for reasonable souls to endue,
   Some made for beasts, some made for birds to wear,
   And all the fruitful spawn of fishes' hue
   In endless ranks along enranged were
That seemed the ocean could not contain them there.

Daily they grow, and daily forth are sent
   Into the world it to replenish more:
   Yet is the stock not lessened, nor spent,
   But still remains in everlasting store
   As it at first created was of yore.
   For in the wide womb of the world there lies,
   In hateful darkness and in deep horror,
   An huge eternal Chaos which supplies
The substances of Nature's fruitful progenies.

All things from thence do their first being fetch
   And borrow matter, whereof they are made
   Which, whenas form and feature it does catch,
   Becomes a body and doth then invade
   The state of life out of the grisly shade.
50   That substance is etern', and bideth so;

Ne when the life decays and form does fade
    Doth it consume and into nothing go,
But changed is, and often altered to and fro.

38

The substance is not changed, nor altered,
    But the only form and outward fashion;
    For every substance is conditioned
    To change her hue and sundry forms to don,
    Meet for her temper and complexion.
    For forms are variable, and decay
    By course of kind and by occasion,
    And that fair flower of beauty fades away
As doth the lily fresh before the sunny ray.

39

Great enemy to it, and to all the rest,
    That in the Garden of Adonis springs
    Is wicked Time, who, with his scythe addressed,
    Does mow the flowering herbs and goodly things
    And all their glory to the ground down flings,
    Where they do wither and are foully marred.
    He flies about and, with his flaggy wings,
    Beats down both leaves and buds without regard,
Ne ever pity may relent his malice hard.

40

Yet pity often did the gods relent
    To see so fair things marred and spoiled quite,
    And their great mother, Venus, did lament

The loss of her dear brood, her dear delight:
   Her heart was pierced with pity at the sight
   When, walking through the garden, them she spied,
   Yet n'ote she find redress for such despite.
   For all that lives, is subject to that law:
All things decay in time, and to their end do draw.

41

But were it not that Time their troubler is,
   All that in this delightful garden grows
   Should happy be and have immortal bliss:
   For here all plenty and all pleasure flows,
   And sweet love gentle fits amongst them throws
   Without fell rancour or fond jealousy,
   Frankly each paramour his leman knows,
   Each bird his mate, ne any does envy
Their goodly merriment and gay felicity.

42

There is continual spring, and harvest there
   Continual, both meeting at one time;
   For both the boughs do laughing blossoms bare
   And with fresh colours deck the wanton prime;
   And eke at once the heavy trees they climb
   Which seem to labour under their fruits' load –
   The whiles the joyous birds make their pastime
   Amongst the shady leaves (their sweet abode)
And their true loves without suspicion tell abroad.

Right in the middest of that Paradise,
   There stood a stately mount, on whose round top
   A gloomy grove of myrtle trees did rise,
   Whose shady boughs sharp steel did never lop,
   Nor wicked beasts their tender buds did crop,
   But, like a garland, compassed the height
   And, from their fruitful sides, sweet gum did drop
   That all the ground, with precious dew bedight,
Threw forth most dainty odours and most sweet delight.

And in the thickest covert of that shade
   There was a pleasant arbour – not by art,
   But of the trees' own inclination made,
   Which, knitting their rank branches part to part,
   With wanton ivy twine entrailed athwart
   And Eglantine and caprifole among,
   Fashioned above within their inmost part,
   That neither Phoebus' beams could through them throng
Nor Aeolus' sharp blast could work them any wrong.

And all about grew every sort of flower
   To which sad lovers were transformed of yore:
   Fresh Hyacinthus (Phoebus' paramour
   And dearest love);
   Foolish Narciss' that likes the watery shore;

Sad Amaranthus, made a flower but late –
Sad Amaranthus, in whose purple gore
Meseems I see Amintas' wretched fate,
To whom sweet poet's verse hath given endless date.

46

There wont fair Venus often to enjoy
  Her dear Adonis' joyous company,
  And reap sweet pleasure of the wanton boy:
  There yet, some say, in secret he does lie,
  Lapped in flowers and precious spicery,
  By her hid from the world, and from the skill
  Of Stygian gods, which do her love envy:
  But she herself, whenever that she will,
Possesseth him and of his sweetness takes her fill.

47

And sooth it seems they say – for he may not
  For ever die and ever buried be
  In baleful night, where all things are forgot:
  Albe he subject to mortality,
  Yet is etern' in mutability
  And by succession made perpetual –
  Transformed oft, and changed diversely;
  For him the Father of all Forms they call:
Therefore needs mote he live, that living gives to all.

A Note on Edmund Spenser

EDMUND SPENCER (c. 1552–99), English poet, born in London, the son of a Lancashire clothmaker who had moved to the capital. The first great modern English poet, Spenser was educated at Merchant Taylor's School, then a grammar school, under Dr Mulcaster. In 1568 he was admitted as sizar at Pembroke Hall, Cambridge. Little is known of his career at Cambridge, but he took his master's degree in 1576, though his Latin composition was apparently poor, and his classical learning copious but inaccurate.

By 1579 Spenser was in London once more, had become acquainted with Sir Philip Sidney and his circle, and obtained a post in the household of Sidney's uncle, the Earl of Leicester. With Sir Philip Sidney, Dyer, and others, he formed a literary club, the Areopagus. In London Spenser came to realise his powers as a poet. At the age of 27 he had already in his mind the outlines of his *Faerie Queene*, and may perhaps have written some portion of it. Shortly after moving to Leicester House he published (1579) the *Shepheardes Calender*, which was well received. In the following year he was appointed secretary to Lord Grey de Wilton, then going as lord deputy to Ireland. Spenser remained in Ireland, holding various posts, until within a month of his death, though he paid occasional visits to England.

In Ireland he was visited by Sir Walter Raleigh, who was his neighbour at Kilcolman, and the visit had important results. For he now renewed the old pastoral form of the *Shepheardes Calender*, and described, under his customary poetic disguise, the circumstances which once more transported him back from Ireland to the court, the goal of all who wished to make their way in the world. This poem, *Colin Clout's Come Home Again*, contains, besides history, criticism, satire, and love passages, the interruption of his retired and 'pastoral' life by the appearance of Raleigh, the 'Shepherd of the Ocean'. At Kilcolman Raleigh became acquainted with Spenser's work on the *Faerie Queene*, and his penetrating judgment told him how far it was in advance of any preceding English poetry. Raleigh's visit thus led directly to the publication of Spenser's masterpiece. Previously Spenser had written an elegy on Sir Philip Sidney (*Astrophel*), who died in 1586. It was three years later that he completed the first three books of the *Faerie Queene*, which had actually been started as early as 1579, and the next three books appeared in 1596.

In 1595 Spenser published *Amoretti* and *Epithalamion*, celebrating his courtship and marriage to his second wife, Elizabeth Boyle. *Amoretti* is one of the most distinguished of the Elizabethan sonnet sequences, with a fine balance of sensuous passion and idealisation. The *Epithalamion* is a richly ornate marriage ode in the classical manner, and the finest of its type in the language. Another marriage ode, *Prothalamion*, for the daughters of the Earl of Worcester, appeared in the following year.

Spenser's lasting claim to fame rests on the unfinished *Faerie Queene*. In the *Letter to Sir Walter Ralegh*, published in the 1590 edition of the poem, he explains that the work is 'a continued Allegory, or darke conceit'. In the person of Prince Arthur he intends to portray 'the image of a brave knight, perfected in the twelve private moral vertues'. While Arthur was to embody all twelve virtues, each of the planned twelve books was to depict one of Gloriana's knights as the special guardian of a particular virtue. Arthur has a vision of the Faerie Queene, Gloriana, in whom, says Spenser, 'I conceive the most excellent and glorious person of our soveraigne the Queene, and her kingdome in Faery land'. So the allegory comprehends a celebration of Elizabeth and her court, England (and more particularly Protestant England, embattled against Catholic Spain), and at the same time an examination of chivalric virtue and romantic passion.

While the references in certain passages are not always easy to define precisely, the narrative is simple to follow in general terms and the language is richly evocative in its distinctive stanzaic form (nine lines, eight iambic pentameters, closing with an alexandrine, and rhyming ababbcbcc, the Spenserian stanza) of Spenser's own invention. The six completed books of the poem contain the exploits of: The Knight of the Red Crosse (Holinesse); Sir Guyon (Temperaunce); Britomart (Chastitie); Cambel and Triamond (Friendship); Artegall (Justice); and Sir Calidore (Courtesie). There are also 'Two Cantos of Mutabilitie' which were part of a projected 'Legend of Constancie' and were not published until 1609.

Other titles in this series